HISTORIC COMMUNITIES

Schoolyard Games

Bobbie Kalman & Heather Levigne

Illustrated by Barbara Bedell

🌳 Crabtree Publishing Company

www.crabtreebooks.com

HISTORIC

COMMUNITIES

Created by Bobbie Kalman

For Papa,
the strongest tree in the forest

Editor-in-Chief
Bobbie Kalman

Writing team
Bobbie Kalman
Heather Levigne

Managing editor
Lynda Hale

Editors
Hannelore Sotzek
Amanda Bishop
Niki Walker

Computer design
Lynda Hale

Production coordinator
Hannelore Sotzek

Special thanks to
Colonial Williamsburg Foundation, Genessee Country Museum,
Black Creek Pioneer Village/TRCA, Leigh Adamson, Brian Adamson,
Jaimie Carini, Lisa Cooper

Photographs
Black Creek Pioneer Village/TRCA: pages 5 (top), page 8 (top), 17 (top right),
18; Colonial Williamsburg Foundation: page 17 (bottom); Marc Crabtree at
Genessee Country Museum: pages 16 (top), 21 Bobbie Kalman at Black Creek
Pioneer Village: page 16 (bottom); Bobbie Kalman at Genessee Country
Museum: page 32; George Ross: cover, page 22; David Schimpky at
Genessee Country Museum: pages 17 (top left), 20

Illustrations
Barbara Bedell: front cover, title page, pages 3 (top left, bottom), 4 (bottom),
   6–7, 9, 10, 12–13, 14, 15, 21, 23 (top), 24, 25, 26, 27, 28–29
John Mantha: back cover
Sarah Pallek: page 20
Bonna Rouse: title page (frogs), pages 3 (all except top left and bottom),
   4 (top), 5, 8, 10–11 (border), 11, 12–13 (border), 18, 19, 22, 23 (bottom), 30

Crabtree Publishing Company

Printed in Canada/092010/DO20100826

PMB 59051
350 Fifth Avenue,
59ᵗʰ Floor
New York, New
York 10118
USA

616 Welland Avenue
St. Catharines,
ON, L2M 5V6
Canada

Maritime House
Basin Road North,
Hove
BN41 1WR
United Kingdom

Cataloging-in-Publication Data
Kalman, Bobbie, 1947-
   Schoolyard games

p. cm.—(Historic communities series)
Includes index.
ISBN 0-86505-441-X (library bound) ISBN 0-86505-471-1 (pbk.)
This book examines the different types of outdoor schoolyard games,
including dodgeball, tag, and skipping, as well as recess activities
played by children in the 19th century North America.

1. Outdoor games—North America—History—19th century—Juvenile
literature. [1. Games—History—19th century.] I. Levigne, Heather. II.
Title. III. Series: Kalman, Bobbie. Historic communities.

LB3031 .K34 2001   j796' .0973'09034—dc21   LC 96-26737
                                                    CIP

Contents

Old-time schoolyard games

In the days of the settlers, children studied at home or attended small one-room schools in which students of all ages learned together. Since most families lived miles apart, children who attended school felt fortunate to be able to meet their friends daily. They especially loved playing games with their classmates in the schoolyard. At home there were many chores to do, leaving little time for play.

Not "It!"

In many schoolyard games, one person was chosen to be **It**. Whoever was It had to chase, tag, or seek the other players. Most children did not want to be It! When someone suggested playing a game such as Hide-and-Seek, children began shouting, "Not It!" The last person who was heard saying "not It" became It for that game.

Who's It?

Children also decided who was It by standing in a circle and holding out their fists. One person recited a rhyme and tapped each player's fists, one after another, to the beat. When the rhyme ended, the last person to have a hand tapped was out. Eventually, all the players but one were eliminated. The last person holding out a fist became It.

One potato, two potato, three potato, four. Five potato, six potato, seven potato, more.

Settler children used this simple rhyme to "count out" players and decide who would be It for a game. The person whose hand was tapped on the word "more" was out. The rhyme continued until one person was left, and that person was It.

Make up your own "count-out" rhymes

Count-out rhymes are easy to make up. Here is another counting rhyme you can use to decide who is It. The person whose hand is tapped on the word "lie" answers "no" or "yes."

As I went up the apple tree,

All the apples fell on me,

Bake a pudding, bake a pie,

Did you ever tell a lie?

N-O spells "no" (or Y-E-S spells "yes")

And you are OUT!

Centuries of games

Settler children played games and sports that had been popular for hundreds of years. Today, children still play schoolyard games such as tag, Hide-and-Seek, and hopscotch. Over time, children have changed some of the rules and given new names to many of the games. Some games still have the same rules, but children in different cities or countries call them by other names.

Recess was a favorite part of the school day. Settler children played games such as tag, Hide-and-Seek, and marbles.

The younger children in a pioneer school played singing games such as "London Bridge" or "Ring Around the Rosie."

Catch me if you can!

Tag games have one thing in common—chasing! They are great for getting rid of energy after sitting at a desk for hours. In most games, one person is It and must chase the other players. As soon as It **tags**, or touches, someone, the tagged person becomes It.

Tiger in the Corner

Five people play this game of tag. Four people stand to make corners of a large square. The fifth person is the "Tiger," who stands in the center. When the Tiger shouts, "Tiger wants a corner!" the other players must switch corners. The Tiger tries to run to a corner before one of the other players does. If the Tiger gets there first, the player who lost a corner becomes the new Tiger.

Red Lion

In this game, one person is the "Lion" and another person is the "Lion's Keeper." The Lion selects an area to be a "den" and stands in that spot. The Lion's Keeper stands nearby. The rest of the players walk slowly toward the den and chant, "Red Lion, Red Lion, come out of your den. Whoever you catch will be one of your friends." When the players get close, the Keeper shouts, "Loose!" and the Lion runs out to chase everyone except the Lion's Keeper. If the Lion catches someone, s/he must say "Red Lion" three times while holding the tagged player. The tagged player becomes a Lion, and the Lions return to the den. Both players now chase the others. The game continues until all the players have been caught.

Sticky Apple can be a very funny game! When you are tagged, you must put one hand on the spot where you were touched. Running while holding a hard-to-reach spot, such as your knee or ankle, is not easy to do!

Everybody hide!

Hiding games are still popular today because no equipment or skills are needed to play. In most hiding games, one player is the seeker while the rest of the players are hiders. Some games, however, are played with only one hider, and everyone else searches for that person. There were few hiding places in a settler schoolyard. Where would you hide in your schoolyard?

Hide-and-Seek

Hide-and-Seek can be played indoors or outdoors, as long as there are enough hiding places. The players decide on a spot to be **home** or **home base**. The player who is It closes his or her eyes and counts up to a number such as 50 or 100, while the rest of the players hide. When It finishes counting, s/he yells, "Ready or not, here I come!" and begins looking for the hidden players.

Home free!

When It finds someone, It shouts "One, two, three on (player's name)," and both players run back to home base. If the hider gets to home base first, s/he shouts "One, two, three, home free!" That player is now safe, and It must look for the other players. If It reaches home first, the player who was caught becomes the new It in the next game. Players do not have to wait to be found before they race home—they can sneak home when It is not looking. The game continues until all the players have been caught or have made it home safely. If no players get caught, the same person is It in the next game.

The person who is It counts to a high number in order to give the other children enough time to find a good hiding spot.

Whoop!

Many years ago, the game of Hide-and-Seek was also known as Whoop. The seeker did not count to 100. Instead, when the hiders were ready, they called out "Whoop!"

Sardines

To play Sardines, one person hides while the rest count. When a seeker finds the hider, s/he must hide in the same place without being spotted by the other seekers. Eventually, all but one of the seekers end up crammed into the hiding spot—just like sardines in a tightly packed can! The first seeker to find the hiding spot is the hider in the new game.

Kick the Can

Players draw a circle on the ground about six feet (2 m) wide and place an empty can in the center. A shoe can also be used. The person who is It must guard the can. The rest of the players stand outside the circle. Suddenly, one person runs into the circle and kicks the can. As It retrieves the can, the rest of the players run and hide. When It returns to the circle, s/he shouts "Freeze!" The players must stop immediately and stay there. It calls out the names of the players s/he can see, and they must stand near the circle as "prisoners." Then It has to find the rest of the players. When It leaves the circle, however, a hider can run in and kick the can again to free the prisoners.

If there are no prisoners, a hiding player can run into the circle and shout "Home free!" All the players then run into the circle. The last player to get inside the circle after "Home free!" is called becomes It for the new game.

In this game of Sardines, the hiding spot is not concealing all the hiders very well! How many children can you see?

Hopping games

Hopping games were easy to play, so both young and older children were able to play them. In winter, children played hopping games to keep warm during recess.

Leapfrog

To play Leapfrog, all the players line up in a row with one player behind the other. The first person in the row bends over in a crouched position called a **back**. The next person in line puts his or her hands on the first person's back and leaps over. Then s/he makes a back in front of that player. The next leaper jumps over the first and second backs, one at a time, like a frog. Play continues with each new leaper jumping over the others until s/he reaches the front of the line. The last person in line then leaps over all the other players. The game continues as long as the "frogs" keep hopping!

Keep the Kettle Boiling

This game is a fast version of Leapfrog. As soon as a player jumps over another player's back, s/he crouches down to make a back for the next person. The person over whom s/he has leapt, immediately stands up and leaps over the person in front. Many players jump at the same time to keep this game moving quickly.

*When making a back, keep your head tucked under to avoid getting hurt. To make a **low back**, crouch down and hold onto your ankles. For a **little back**, get down on your hands and knees. Leaning forward with your hands on your knees, as shown left, makes a **high back**.*

Hopscotch

Hopscotch is a very old game that dates back to ancient Rome. Romans etched their grids into stone floors, but the settlers drew them on the ground. To play, each player needs a throwing piece called a **potsie** or **pitcher**. You can use a small stone or even your shoe as the potsie.

Let's get hopping!

To start, a player stands at the beginning of the hopscotch grid and throws the potsie into the first square. S/he hops on one foot from one end of the grid to the other, without landing on the square that contains the marker or stepping on the lines. On single squares, a player hops on one foot. On each double square, however, s/he can land with one foot in each square. When s/he reaches the end of the grid, the player turns around on the last square and hops back to the beginning. On the way back, s/he must stop in the second block and pick up the potsie from the first one. Then s/he throws it into the second square and hops from beginning to end again, avoiding the potsie.

Watch your step!

A player continues until s/he makes a mistake such as throwing the marker into the wrong block or onto a line, or putting down both feet in a single square. Then the next player takes a turn. At the end of each turn, the potsies stay where they have landed, and the upcoming players must avoid every square that contains one. When it is their turn again, players start where they left off. The game continues until each player has thrown his or her potsie into the last square and has hopped from one end of the grid to the other and back.

Draw your hopscotch grid as shown here. Remember to number each square! You can scratch the grid into the dirt, as settler children did, or draw it on pavement using a piece of chalk.

Skipping games

Skipping was originally a game that boys played, but it later became a game mainly for girls. Settler children made their own skipping ropes out of grapevines, **hop stems**, or braided straw.

Bringing spring in with a jump

Skipping was also a popular activity on May Day, when people celebrated the coming of spring. In May, settlers planted crops such as corn, potatoes, and wheat. They believed that jumping during planting season would help the crops grow. The higher they jumped, the taller the plants would grow!

For these two rhymes, turn the rope as fast as possible during the last sentence. Change the names to the names of your classmates.

Down by the river where the green grass grows,
There sits Amanda, pretty as a rose,
Along comes Peter and kisses her on the cheek,
How many kisses did she get this week?
One, two, three, four...

Bluebells, cockleshells,
Eevy, ivy, over,
My mother sent me to the store,
And this is what she sent me for—
Salt, mustard, vinegar, pepper!

In this skipping rhyme, skippers make the actions described in each line. When spelling "good night," the rope is turned as fast as possible while the skipper tries to spell the entire word without tripping.

Grizzly bear, grizzly bear, turn around.
Grizzly bear, grizzly bear, touch the ground.
Grizzly bear, grizzly bear, shine your shoes.
Grizzly bear, grizzly bear, read the news.
Grizzly bear, grizzly bear, go upstairs.
Grizzly bear, grizzly bear, say your prayers.
Grizzly bear, grizzly bear, blow out the light.
Grizzly bear, grizzly bear, spell good night—
G-O-O-D N-I-G-H-T!

Skipping terms:
salt Turn the rope slowly
mustard or **vinegar** Turn the rope at normal speed
pepper Turn the rope as fast as you can
bluebells or **rock the cradle** Swing the rope from side to side but not all the way around
high water Hold the rope high so it does not touch the ground as you turn it
low water Crouch down and turn the rope so the skipper must skip in a crouched position
chase the fox Everyone follows the leader, who runs in and out of the rope
under the moon Players run under the turning rope without skipping
over the stars Players run and jump over the rope

Let's play ball!

Ball games were very popular among the settlers. Most of the balls used were made of wood, cork, or stuffed leather. They were very heavy and did not bounce. The first bouncing balls were made from bull bladders that were filled with air and covered with leather. These balls were hard, however, so any contact they made with the body was painful. In 1839, toymakers began using rubber to make softer, bouncier balls for children's games such as Dodge Ball.

Baseball

Baseball is one of most popular sports in North America. It is based on a game called **rounders**, which was played by the British settlers in the 1700s. In rounders, players used a stick to hit a rock and then ran around three posts. In the 1800s, people began using bats, balls, and bases to play this game, which soon became known as baseball.

In early baseball games, players did not wear leather gloves—they caught the ball with their bare hands!

Nine Holes

Each player digs a small hole near a wall, and a line is drawn about sixteen feet (5 m) away from the holes. Each player stands near a hole, except one player, who is the pitcher. The pitcher stands on the line and throws a soft ball into one of the holes. When s/he gets the ball into a hole, everyone runs away, except the person to whom the hole belongs. This person grabs the ball and throws it at one of the fleeing players.

The person who gets hit with the ball becomes the pitcher for the next game. If the thrower misses, however, s/he becomes the pitcher. A player is out of the game after missing three times. The winner is the last person to remain in the game.

Dodge Ball

To play Dodge Ball, players divide into two teams. One team forms a large circle, and the other team stands inside the circle. One person on the team forming the circle starts the game by throwing the ball at a player inside the circle. To prevent anyone from getting hurt, players must aim the ball below the knees and try to hit the other team members on the legs. The players inside the circle move quickly to dodge the ball!

When a player is hit, s/he joins the other team and becomes part of the circle. The game continues until all the players inside the circle have been tagged with the ball. To make Dodge Ball more challenging, try playing with two balls!

Aim below the knees, please!

Homemade toys

All children love to bring their toys to school. Settler children, however, did not own many store-bought toys because most families could not afford them. Materials for toys and games had to be inexpensive and easy to find or make. Some children owned a few basic items such as hoops, balls, marbles, tops, and jump ropes. Older children were able to make some of their own toys such as kites and beanbags.

(above) Settler children played checkers on handmade wooden boards. The checkers were often made of dried, sliced corncobs.

Dolls
Fancy dolls made of wax or porcelain were expensive. Very few pioneer girls owned these types of dolls. Instead, most girls had dolls that were handmade from rags or cornhusks. Girls who owned fancy china dolls did not bring them to school because these dolls broke easily and were costly and difficult to replace. Many children brought rag dolls, which were more durable, to school.

Wooden toys
Today, most toys are made of **synthetic** materials such as plastic. The toys of settler children were made of natural materials such as cotton, dried plant fibers, and wood. Wood was used to make hoops, stilts, building blocks, tops, **whirligigs**, and **Jacob's Ladders**, which are shown on page 32. Many older children learned how to **whittle**, or carve, their own toys. The girl on the next page has mastered the skill of walking on homemade wooden stilts.

(left) This girl is playing with a wooden whirligig. A large button and string also worked well. Spinning a whirligig provided hours of fun.

(above) Corn was a basic food for the pioneers. After the corn was harvested, the husks were dried and used to make dolls for children.

(right) These boys are playing with a toy called an **acrobat**. Squeezing the handles at the bottom pulls the string taut and makes the wooden figure jump, twist, and turn somersaults!

String games

The only equipment needed to play string games is a piece of string about five feet (1.5 m) long. Players take turns looping the strings around each other's fingers. In some string games, players use their toes and teeth to pull the strings around their fingers! These pages show how to play Cat's Cradle.

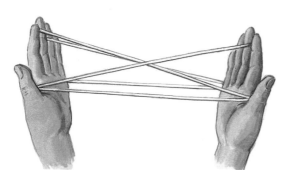

To start Cat's Cradle, loop the string around the back of both your hands and pass it through the space between your thumbs and index fingers. Loop the string around each hand again so it crosses your palms. Slide each middle finger under the loop on the palm of the opposite hand. Separate your hands. You will have two crossed strings with one straight string on either side, making the Cat's Cradle design.

Native American string games

For hundreds of years, Native Americans have used string to make pictures and tell stories. They often sat around a fire and made string figures of animals such as bears, coyotes, and caribou. While they made the string figures, they sang songs or told stories and legends about these animals.

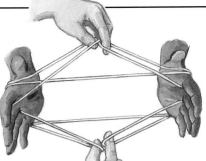

1. Pinch the crisscrossed strings. Pull them out to each side and then under the straight strings.

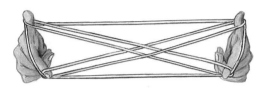

2. After pulling the strings through, spread your thumbs and index fingers wide apart. This string figure is called the Soldier's Bed.

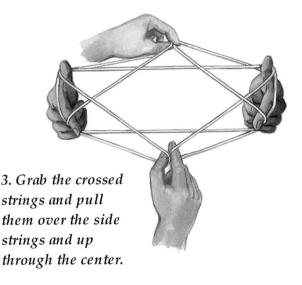

3. Grab the crossed strings and pull them over the side strings and up through the center.

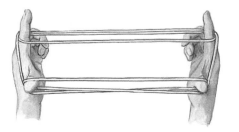

4. Separate your thumbs and index fingers to make Candles. The parallel strings resemble two long, tapered candles.

5. Pick up the inside "candle" strings with each little finger. Pull each to the opposite side. With the strings still hooked over your pinkies, draw them over the outside strings and up through the center.

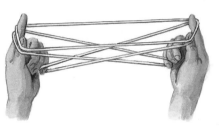

6. This figure is called the Manger. You should still be holding strings on each pinkie finger.

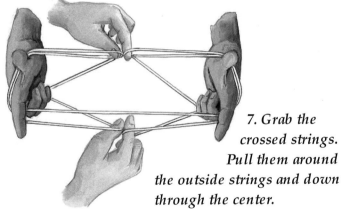

7. Grab the crossed strings. Pull them around the outside strings and down through the center.

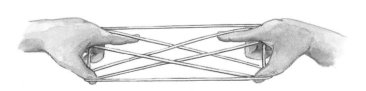

8. Your fingers should point downward to make Diamonds, which looks like the Soldier's Bed. What do you think is the next step?

Whirling, twirling tops

Tops provided settler children with hours of spinning fun! A top is a toy with a wide top and narrow bottom and an iron peg through the center. To spin tops, players wound a string around the peg. They threw their top on the ground while holding one end of the string in their hand. They pulled the string to unwind it, which caused the top to spin.

Peg-in-the-Ring

To play this game, children drew a circle on the ground about three feet (1 m) wide. Players threw their tops into the ring one at a time, trying to **peg**, or hit, the other tops in the ring. The object of the game was to split an opponent's top and keep the iron peg as a trophy.

If a player threw a top and it did not spin or stopped spinning, the top was called "dead." The player could not pick it up to throw it again. Since a dead top was easier to hit than a spinning one, the other players threw their tops at it. If a player pegged a dead top and it bounced outside the ring, it became "live" again. The owner was then allowed to rejoin the game and throw his or her top at the other tops.

Conqueror

Conqueror was an exciting game! Two players spun their tops so that the tops bounced against each other. The top that knocked the other over, but stayed upright itself, was the winner.

Fun with hoops

Wooden hoops were often used in pioneer children's games. The town **cooper**, or barrel maker, often gave children the old barrel hoops to use for their games. The wheelwright and blacksmith provided metal hoops from old tires.

Hoop and stick

Using a stick, children rolled a hoop along the ground as fast as they could. Some children mastered a single hoop and then learned to roll two or more hoops at once! Sometimes they had hoop races to see who could keep their hoop rolling the fastest or longest.

Through the Hoop

In this competitive game, one person rolled a hoop in a straight line along the ground while one or more players stood about fifteen feet (4.5 m) away. The standing players tried to throw their stick through the hoop as it rolled past them. The winner was the player who tossed his or her stick through the hoop the greatest number of times without knocking it down.

(above) Learning how to keep the hoop rolling in a straight line took practice!

Graces

Girls often played Graces, or Grace Hoops, shown right. They developed their balance and coordination by playing this game. Players used sticks to toss a small hoop to each other. They tried to keep the hoop from touching the ground. Catching the hoop on the stick was difficult! To make the game more challenging, girls often played Graces using two hoops, catching both hoops on their stick at once.

Marbles come in many sizes, patterns, and colors. Do you have any marbles that look like these?

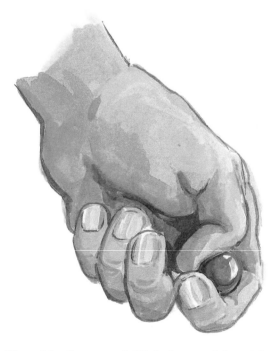

Knuckle down and flick the marble with your thumb, as shown above.

Marble madness!

Marble games were popular with people of all ages. In the 1800s, almost every child owned a bag of favorite marbles for playing games in the schoolyard. Marbles have interesting names such as "cat's eyes," "swirls," "onionskins," and "clouds."

Many kinds of marbles

Some types of early marbles were made of stones that were polished until they were round and smooth. Homemade marbles called **marrididdles** were made of clay. They were left to dry in the sun until they hardened. Other types of marbles were made of wood, steel, glass, and china. **Aggies** were made of **agate**, which is a hard mineral. Clear marbles called **sulfides** contained tiny carvings of animals or objects.

Marble games

Marble games are divided into three basic types: chase, circle, and hole games. In chase and circle games, players shoot at one another's marbles in a specific area such as a circle drawn on flat ground. In hole games, players shoot their marbles into a hole dug in the ground.

Shooting marbles

To shoot a marble, point your hand down and curl your fingers into your palm. Tuck your thumb behind your index finger. Place a marble in the space between your thumb and finger and **knuckle down**, or rest the knuckle of your index finger on the ground. Flick out your thumb to shoot the marble. Some games require players to use a slightly larger marble for shooting and hitting an opponent's marbles.

Ring Taw

To play Ring Taw, draw a circle about three feet (1 m) wide on the ground and have each player put several marbles inside. Then draw a larger circle about six feet (2 m) wide outside the smaller one. Players choose a starting point on the outer circle from which they will make their first shot.

One person knuckles down and tries to hit a marble inside the ring with a **taw**, or shooting marble. If s/he knocks out a marble and the taw also goes out of the ring, that player keeps the marble that was hit. S/he now knuckles down again from the spot where the taw landed.

If a player misses and the taw rolls out of the inner ring, s/he shoots from that spot on his or her next turn. If s/he hits a marble or misses, but his or her taw stays inside the ring, s/he can get back the taw by replacing it with another marble. Players do not like to lose their favorite taw!

Ring Taw is a popular marble game. In the picture above, the player is knuckling down before shooting his marble into the ring.

Boss-out

Boss-out, or Hits and Spans, is a simple marble game. Children often played this chasing game on the way to school because it made a long walk much more fun! Only two people are needed to play this game, but more can play.

The first player throws a marble ahead a few feet. The second player then shoots his or her marble. If it hits the first player's marble or lands within a **span** of it, s/he wins it. A span is the distance between a player's outstretched thumb and index finger. If the second player does not hit or span the first player's marble, then it is the first player's turn to try and hit that player's marble.

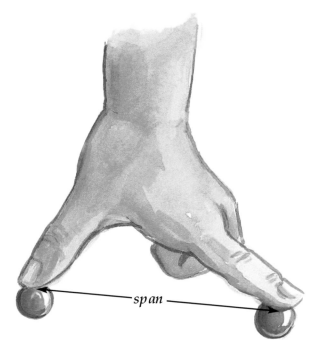

Be fair when measuring a span—do not stretch your fingers too far apart.

Winter fun

In some areas, winter was a long, cold season. People had more time for leisure activities because they did not have to plant or harvest crops, repair buildings or farm equipment, or herd livestock. Playing games kept people entertained during the winter.

Fun in the snow
Children did not let snow stop them from playing games at recess. Some of their favorite games and activities could be played only in the winter.

Children looked forward to the first snowfall. On sunny days, they played outdoor games of tag such as Fox and Geese. Tobogganing, ice skating, and ice shinny were other fun winter activities. Which are your favorite winter games?

Many winter schoolyard games kept children warm. Skating, sledding, and running were physical activities that helped keep children active and healthy during the winter months.

Tobogganing

Tobogganing was a popular winter recess activity. Children dragged their wooden toboggans behind them on their way to school. When the recess bell rang, they rushed outside to the nearest snow-covered hill or slope. Sliding downhill was exciting! A rope handle was used to help steer the toboggan downhill and pull it uphill.

Fox and Geese

Fox and Geese is a game of tag played in the snow. Using their feet, players mark a large circle in the snow with a smaller circle in the center. Several paths lead out from the inner circle to the outer one, like the spokes of a wheel. The center circle is the "safe" area. One player is the "fox," and the rest of the players are "geese." The fox tries to catch the geese, who must stay on the paths. The geese can run into the center, but if they stay too long, they become trapped! When a goose is tagged, s/he becomes the new fox.

Ice shinny

Native Americans played an outdoor sport called **shinny**, which was the basis for the game of hockey that we play today. In summer they played on a grassy field, and in winter they played on a frozen river or lake. The teams were made up of ten to 50 players. Each player had a long curved stick that s/he used to hit a puck made of rawhide-covered wood or stone. Two logs were placed 130 feet (40 m) apart and were used as goal posts. To score goals, each team tried to shoot the puck between the other team's posts.

Some toboggans were large enough to allow several people to ride downhill at the same time.

Indoor recess games

In rainy or very cold weather, students did not go outside during recess. Staying indoors could be just as much fun as playing outside. Children played guessing games, word games, and indoor versions of their favorite outdoor recess games.

Hot Buttered Beans

Nobody hides in this hiding game, but something is "hidden." While the rest of the players cover their eyes, one person places a small object such as a thimble where it is visible but hard to see. When the thimble is placed, the player who hid it calls out, "Hot buttered beans! Please come to supper!" The rest of the players then uncover their eyes and search for the thimble. When players are far from it, the hider says, "Cold." When they get close to the thimble, s/he calls out, "Warm." As the seekers get closer, the hider tells them that they are "warmer." When the searching players are very close, the hider says, "Hot!" The person who finds the thimble hides it the next time.

I Spy

I Spy is a searching game that is similar to Hot Buttered Beans. To play, one person looks around the room and selects an object but does not tell the rest of players what it is. The person gives a clue to the players about the object. S/he might say, "I spy with my little eye something that is red." The other children then take turns guessing what the mystery object is by looking for things that are red. Use the clues on this page to find the objects in the picture on the opposite page. Make up some clues of your own and have a friend guess the names of other objects that you have "spied."

Gossip is played by a group of people. One person whispers a sentence into another player's ear, who then whispers it into the next player's ear. The last person who hears the sentence says it out loud. Often, the final version of the original sentence is not only different but also very funny!

I SPY IN
THE
GENERAL STORE

I spy something that is eaten with eggs.
I spy something that has four legs.
I spy something that looks like my mother.
I spy something that is on my brother.

I spy something that contains a pickle.
I spy something you can buy for a nickel.
I spy something with a round pot belly.
I spy something that is eaten with jelly.

(Turn to page 31 for the answers)

Ready, set, go!

On the last day of school, many schools held a field day. Parents, teachers, and students brought food for a picnic lunch. Later, they held different types of races and played games such as baseball. Racing games such as Egg-in-the-Spoon, Push the Potato, and the Three-legged Race were very popular.

Push the Potato

For this race, each player needs a potato to push along the ground. All the players line up in a row. At the starting signal, they begin rolling their potato along the ground with their nose. Players may use only their nose—never their hands—to keep the potato rolling in a straight line. The first person who crosses the finish line wins the race.

Is this player going to use her right hand to push the potato? What do you think?

Three-legged Race

For the Three-legged Race, everyone needs a partner. Tie your right leg to your partner's left leg with a rope. You can also put your right leg into a burlap sack while your partner puts his or her left leg into the sack. When the starter yells, "Go!" you and your partner must run as fast as you can without tripping or falling down. Keeping the same stride as that of your partner is difficult!

Ready, set, go!

Egg-in-the-Spoon

Each player places an egg on a spoon and lines up in a row. At the starting signal, everyone begins running toward the finish line while balancing their egg on the spoon. It is hard to keep the egg on the spoon while running! The winner is the first person to cross the finish line with the egg still on the spoon.

Watch the egg, and it won't drop out!

Clap your hands

Clapping games were popular with settler children. Each game had a different clapping pattern to go with its own song or rhyme. Many clapping games were tricky and difficult to master. Settler girls played clapping games that required good coordination. As they practiced, they were able to clap and sing very quickly. Play the clapping game below as fast as you can.

Miss Mary Mac

For this rhyme, repeat the last word of each sentence three times as you clap both of your hands on your partner's hands three times. The verses are below the illustrations.

Miss ⟶ Mar- ⟶ -ry ⟶ Mac, Mac, Mac

Miss Mary Mac
All dressed in black
With silver buttons
All down her back.

She asked her mother
For fifteen cents
To see the elephants
Jump over the fence.

They jumped so high
They touched the sky
They didn't come back
Till the end of July!

Glossary

blacksmith A person who shapes iron into objects such as horseshoes

Cat's Cradle A game played with a long piece of string in which two or more players use a series of hand movements to create string designs

cooper A person who makes wooden barrels and buckets

high back A position in Leapfrog in which a player bends forward slightly from the waist and holds his or her knees

home base A place from which a game begins; a game's goal or endpoint

hop stems The long stems of the hop plant, which the settlers used for making jump ropes

Jacob's Ladder A toy made of several flat blocks of wood connected with ribbon, which appear to tumble down when held in the air (see picture on page 32)

knuckle down Describing the position of the hand when preparing to shoot a marble

little back A position in Leapfrog in which a player bends forward and holds onto his or her ankles

low back A position in Leapfrog in which a player gets down on his or her hands and knees

May Day A celebration that takes place on May 1st to mark the coming of spring

one-room school A school building in which all the children were taught in the same room by one teacher

peg (n) The iron spike inside a top; (v) to hit another player's top with your top

potsie An object, such as a small stone or pine cone, that is used as a marker in hopscotch; also called a **pitcher**

rounders An old-fashioned game that was similar to baseball, in which players hit a stick with a rock and ran around posts

shinny In this game, originally played by Native Americans, players use long sticks to hit a ball between two goal posts. Shinny is played on ice or on a field.

span The distance measured between the thumb and index finger

synthetic Describing something that is made from materials not found in nature

taw A player's favorite marble that s/he uses to shoot at the other marbles in a game

top A small wooden toy, narrow at one end and wide at the other, which spins when it is thrown on the ground

wheelwright A person who makes wheels for wagons, carriages, and carts

whirligig A spinning toy made from a length of string threaded through a hole in a round piece of wood

Answers to riddles on page 26:
Ham and sausages are eaten with eggs,
The sleeping cat has four furry legs,
The pretty china figure looks like Mother,
A bright blue cap is worn by my brother.

The stout wooden barrel contains a pickle,
Sweet lollipops cost only a nickel,
The black iron stove has a round pot belly,
Muffins and tarts are eaten with jelly.

Index